Willie the Hippo's A to Z of Animals

Written by Ted Smith
Researched by Elizabeth Smith
Illustrated by Valentina Rinaldi

Copyright Ted Smith 2024, all rights reserved

Published by Edward MR Smith

Copyright © Ted Smith 2024

All rights reserved. No part of this book may be reproduced in any manner whatsoever without written permission except in the case of brief quotations embodied in critical articles and reviews.

First printing 2024

For more information, visit the Facebook fan page 'Willie the Hippo and Friends'

Dedicated to Luka and Marko Smith
Heartfelt thanks to Liz and Valentina for helping make it happen

When all the visitors leave the safari park for the night, Benji, the rabbit, opens the hippo enclosure so Willie can come out to play.

In this book, Willie introduces us to some of the friends that he has made at the park.

For safety reasons, there is no mention of Monkateetee and his gang of monkeys…..

A a Armadillo

Euphractuse sexinctus

Willie first met Alejandro the Armadillo in the lake at the safari park. They competed with each other to see how long they could stay under the water without breathing. Both managed about 5 minutes before they had to surface for fresh air.

Willie was impressed to learn that Armadillo means 'little armoured one' in Spanish and that the armour is made from over-lapping keratin plates.

Alejandro had a great trick: he could inflate his stomach with air and float on the surface!

In a swimming race, they were equally fast, and when they emerged from the water, they realised that they could both jump quite high and run fast. They made lots of mess and created some really stinky mud trying these things out.

Willie learned that over twenty types of Armadillos live in Central and South America. They are omnivores, eating insects, plants, fruit, and eggs. Their long tongues can reach deep inside an ant nest or a termite mound.

Their eyesight and hearing are poor, but they have a great sense of smell. They have claws on their short front legs, and the females lay between 1 and 15 eggs yearly, living up to 10 years old.

B b Brown Bear

Ursus arctos

When the brown bears first arrived at the safari park, Willie was very excited. They had a special enclosure made for them, which included a tree they could climb and a hollow trunk they could sleep in.

When the cubs were born, they were blind, hairless, had no teeth and weighed about 400g. Their mum explained to Willie that she would need to look after them for about three years, teaching them how to hunt and fish, where to make a den and how to fight.

The bears are omnivores, eating some meat but primarily plants, pinecones, fruit and nuts. They love eating bees' nests when they get the chance, being addicted to the sweet honey.

Bears live for up to thirty years and spend most of the winter sleeping (it's not the same as hibernation because they can wake quickly if they hear a worrying sound).

When they stand up on their hind legs, they are taller than a man and pack a powerful punch, which can kill prey in one hit. Their broad paws' claws and pads allow them to run fast on slippery surfaces, sometimes catching slower animals.

They prefer to hunt and search for food around dawn and dusk, but they have been found walking around at all times of the day and night, especially when looking for a mate.

C c Cheetah

Acinonyx jubatus

Willie always thought he was fast when running, but when he learned that the cheetahs could go from 0 to 100 km/h and have been recorded at 128 km/h, he was shocked. That's almost as fast as a car on a motorway.

Cheetahs use that astonishing speed (they are the fastest land animal in the world) to catch antelopes, gazelles, impalas, rabbits and sometimes birds. They are true carnivores, eating meat.

When running very fast and needing to change direction, they use their tail, just like a rudder on a ship, to steer themselves in a different direction. Willie tried to do that, but his tiny tail made no real difference, and he fell over!

Unlike most animals, they have adapted to needing a drink only every three or four days, allowing them to survive for relatively long periods on the plains in Africa and Asia between kills.

Willie learned that the cheetah lived for ten to twelve years.

.

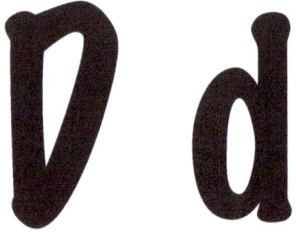  Deer

Cervidae

Willie was impressed that Deer, the only animal in the world with antlers, would visit him at the safari park. Although deer were wild and lived in the nearby woods, they were inquisitive and would often come up to his enclosure in the Spring.

The deer told Willie that their antlers would fall off yearly and re-grow. They said that antlers were the fastest-growing living tissue in the world, wow!

Willie also learned that deer have four stomachs and that the grass and leaves they eat undergo different processes in each stomach until they extract all the nutrients.

The deer also explained that they could usually see people, like the park rangers, coming from quite a distance. They had 310-degree vision, whereas humans had just 180 degrees, and they could see well at night.

Deer can live up to about twenty years old, be as high as 2m, and weigh up to 700kg. They can also jump very high, around 3m, so Willie wondered if they could enter his enclosure. He will ask them next time they visit.

E e   Elephant

Elepantidae

FanFan is Willie's best friend, alongside Benji the rabbit, of course.

FanFan has a really useful trunk. It can pick up heavy things, it can push things, it can hoover up food on the ground, suck up water and pick something as delicate as a flower.

Best of all is that FanFan can trumpet the most extraordinary noises from her trunk, including shouting "Poo Spray Alert!" when Willie goes into attack mode.

FanFan has also been known to suck up peanuts and then shoot them back out, like a machine gun, when the monkeys attack.

Elephants can live up to 60 years and weigh up to 7000kg, which is like a large truck. They eat 150 kilograms of food daily, which is a lot and makes it very expensive to keep them at a safari park.

Willie knew that elephants were very clever. They had learned to use tools and had long memories. They even remembered the unique place where they went to die.

Whereas a human takes nine months before giving birth to a baby, the elephant takes 22 months. Elephants are very protective parents and will do whatever it takes to prevent their babies being hurt.

F f Frigate Bird

Euphractuse sexinctus

Willie was astonished when he first met the Frigate Birds in the aviary and started talking to them. He could sleep while floating in the water, but he could not imagine how a bird could sleep while flying. What if it bumped into something, like a mountain or a tree? What if it started to go in the wrong direction and ended up miles out at sea?

Willie found it challenging to understand, and the birds couldn't explain, but they did flap their wings, which span over 2 metres, and showed how they could glide on the wind currents and conserve energy for when it was needed most.

Willie loved the amazing red throat of the male frigate bird and wanted one for himself. Indeed, the next day, he asked Joffy, the giraffe, to get some red berries from the tree, and he smeared them all over his throat. But it didn't look as effective as the bird because he couldn't expand his throat about ten times its normal size!

Willie learned that males use the red throat to attract females and that once they form a pair, they stay together until the baby has grown up and left them.

The birds also took great care of raising their babies. They had one baby every two years to ensure the baby grew up strong and was always protected by them

Willie liked to eat anything green that lived on the river or pond floor, but these birds preferred to eat fish and squid. At least the safari park had a good supply of fish, so all was well.

G g Giraffe

Giraffa camelopardalis

Willie loved the three young giraffes at the safari park. Jiffy, Joffy, and Jaffy would often play with him in the evenings after the park closed and get into all sorts of trouble. Their necks were amazingly long—over 2 meters long, and one was even 2.5 meters long. That meant they could reach fresh leaves high up on the trees that the other animals could only look at.

It also meant that they could help Willie break into other parts of the park because they could move the bolts at the top of the security gates. And when Willie was doing something naughty, they could act as the lookout for him and spot wardens from a long way away because their eyes were so high up on their heads.

Jiffy, Joffy and Jaffy would sometimes play at fighting, and they did this by swinging their heads from side to side using their long necks and then hitting each other. They always made a big noise when doing this, and Willie had learned to keep out of the way.

Not only did they have long necks, but their tongues were also weird (in Willie's mind). They were dark blue and could stretch over half a meter.

Their bodies were camouflaged to blend into the trees in the background, a handy thing in the savannah of their home country in Africa, where real lions would be trying to find them for their next meal.

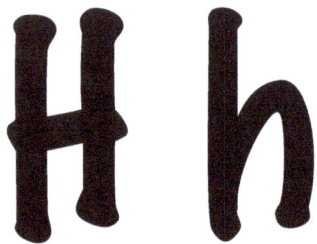

Hippopotamus

Hippopotamus amphibius

Willie asked his Mum and Dad many questions before writing about hippos. He knew, for example, he could hold his breath underwater for 3 minutes, but his dad could easily beat him and had managed five and a half minutes.

Willie could sleep in the water, which was a great trick when the sun was hot and he wanted to keep cool during the day. He had watched his Mum sleeping; her head would rise just out of the water so her nostrils could replace the air in her lungs before sinking again.

Willie's grandparents originally came from Uganda, where they lived on the banks of the Nile, a long and famous African river. The safari park built a big pool and a paddock for Willie to run around. Willie could run as fast as the cars that visited the park, up to 30 km/h. He was slower in the water but still much faster than humans.

Grandad lived until his fiftieth birthday and weighed 3000kg. Willie wanted to beat his record, so he ate good vegetables and grasses, ran and swam daily, and had evening adventures with Benji and FanFan.

Willie used his famous 'Poo Spray' to scare off the monkeys whenever they became troublesome, but his dad had explained that in Africa, he would need to use it to mark out his territory. There were lots of hippos in the big rivers, and they lived in groups called Pods or Bloats, and they would mark their boundaries by flicking poo with their tails. And if ever they were threatened, they would open their giant mouths, spray poo and then charge at the animal threatening them.

Impala

Aepyceros melampus

Willie loved the red-brown coat of the Impala and the lovely slender horns that the males had. He enjoyed springtime, watching the male Impala's fighting to be the leader for several weeks. But even more impressive was their ability to jump. They could jump over each other, something no hippo can do, and they could win the award for best long jump, covering 10 metres in one leap.

The Impala were a great lookout. When the first visitors started arriving at the safari park, the Impala nearly always noticed them first. They would see a car and start snorting and then grunting, a loud noise that could be heard almost 2km away. Most Impalas at the safari park lived until they were at least 15. Still, Willie's dad said they would only live about 12 years in the southern African savannah because cheetahs, lionesses and leopards hunted them.

There were two things that Willie thought were quite funny about Impala. Firstly, they practised social distancing, nearly always keeping a couple of metres apart, and secondly that they loved to spray their poo and wee around everywhere, marking their territory, even though there were no other herds at the safari park.

Jj Jackal

Canis

Willie was pleased that the safari park jackals were kept in a secure enclosure. He knew that they were carnivores who ate small animals, birds and reptiles, and he warned Benji the rabbit, his best friend, to keep well away from them.

Willie had only seen them a few times, but he remembered how big their feet seemed and how straight their legs were. Evolution had designed them to be able to run for long distances when they were hunting their prey at dawn and dusk.

Jackals lived in pairs, staying with their partner for their whole life. They marked their territory with poo and wee, just like Willie, and lived for about ten years.

Near the park café was a statue of Anubis, an ancient Egyptian God, that Willie liked. It always reminded him of the jackals and their pointy heads. Both Anubis and the Jackals originated in Africa.

K k Kangaroo

Euphractuse sexinctus

The kangaroos were real troublemakers at the safari park, even more so than Willie and his friends. They were forever breaking down the fences that kept them in their enclosure by jumping up and kicking them with their powerful feet and legs.

They looked remarkably like a massive version of Benji, the rabbit to Willie. However, they had some significant differences, like the pouch on their tummies that the females kept their babies in for up to nine months. Thus, the zookeepers called them marsupials.

When they escaped from their pen, Willie would watch in awe as they hopped around the main grass area at 40 km/h speeds, easily beating the park rangers on their quad bikes, who couldn't make the roos' violent turns without falling off their bikes. Willie's Dad said that they liked to escape to eat the fresh grass in the central park and to show the rangers who were boss. He said they were strictly herbivores and never ate anything else.

Ll

Lion

Leo

Willie got along well with the lions. He had helped some cubs escape, and they had won their football game against the zebras. He had also saved a lion wedding when he fought off the pesky monkeys trying to disrupt it.

Willie noticed that the female lions always seemed to be the most active. He learned that they would do most of the hunting while the male lions liked to eat and sleep. They regularly ate zebras and giraffes on the African plains, which explained the sizeable electric fence built around their enclosure in the safari park.

Willie loved watching the mothers carry their cubs by picking them up from the neck. The first time he saw them, it looked like the mother was about to eat the cub, which surprised Willie.

The lions ate lots of meat, at least 5kg a day each, which was thrown to them by the zookeepers from a safe lorry. Once, the zookeepers had accidentally left the back of the truck down, and the lions ate all the meat (over 200kg) in one go. Willie's dad said this would be like real life for them on the Savannah when they would only be successful hunting every few days and eat the lot in one sitting.

The lions were quite noisy at night; sometimes, it sounded like they were trying to communicate with the pride of lions in the other safari park, about 100 km away. Willie was pleased he could sleep underwater; otherwise, their noise would wake him.

M m Meerkats

Suricata surucata

Meerkats made Willie laugh. A lot. Every time he saw them in their enclosure (built specially to stop them from burrowing out through tunnels), they would be standing on their hind legs, with their heads swivelling in all directions. They were always on the lookout for predators, even though they were safe in their safari park home. The other thing that made them fun was that baby meerkats always played around. Unlike many animals, they didn't have a mating season, so new babies appeared all year round.

Like Willie, they came from Africa. Unlike Willie, they could change their body temperature depending on the weather, whereas Willie had to get into the water to cool down or warm up, depending upon the season.

The other big difference was that Willie ate vegetation, whilst the meerkats preferred beetles, small birds and reptiles.

N n

Narwhal

Monodon monoceros

When the safari park first opened, it had a pair of narwhals in a big pool specially built for them. They had left the park to be released into the sea near Canada before Willie was born, so he only knew about them from what his Dad told him and the fantastic sculpture next to the big pool, which the rock-hopper penguins now inhabited.

The narwhal is famous for its single large hollow tusk protruding from its head. Willie could understand why some people believed in unicorns; their heads looked similar.

Willie learned that Narwhals are a type of whale. Their babies must be suckled on their mother's milk for twenty months, a long time. They live in groups and feed on fish, sometimes diving for up to 25 minutes to a depth of 1500m. They grow to 5.5m long and can weigh up to 1600kg, the same size and weight as a car.

Narwhals can live up to fifty years old. Most of the year, they swim under the ice packs in the freezing waters around North America and Greenland, coming up for air using small break holes in the ice. But in the summer, they migrate towards the beaches to find mates for breeding.

Orca whales, polar bears, and Inuit humans hunt them.

O o Orang Utan

Pongo pygmaeus

When Willie first heard that the scientific name of the Orangutan was Pongo, he got excited, thinking that they must have stinky poo like his. He was disappointed, but then he learned that 'orang' means a person in the Malaysian language, and 'hutan' means forest. 'Forest person' seemed entirely appropriate, given how much they looked like the park rangers and liked hanging around in the trees.

Just like Willie, they are omnivores, eating all sorts of fruit, leaves and tree bark in the jungle, and they can reach the highest treetops by climbing with their exceptionally long and strong arms (their legs being relatively weak). They like to eat a fruit called Durian, which smells like farts (maybe that is why they are called Pongo, wondered Willie).

After they are born, they stay with their mothers until they are about seven years old. They learn all they need to know, holding onto their mother's body at first and then travelling independently. They live to about 35 in the wild, but some can live to 50 in safari parks and zoos.

They sleep in nests, which they build fresh every night. They make the nest by bending large branches and weaving smaller ones to create a hammock. They also use tools: sticks to remove termites, ants, and bees from holes in the ground or in trees and leaves as gloves when handling prickly fruits.

P p

Polar Bear

Ursus maritimus

Polar Bears live in the wilds of Arctic Canada, Alaska, Greenland, Russia, and Norway. They grow to be 2.5m long and weigh 680kg. Male Polar Bears can weigh as much as ten men. They are the largest carnivores on Earth.

Willie knew all this from reading the sign outside their enclosure at the safari park. He could tell it was true by looking at them in their pen, although he thought their thick fur and layer of blubber might not be so good in a long, hot summer.

Willie was astonished when one of the polar bears told him his skin under the fur was black. He explained that the fur is translucent and only appears white to everyone as it reflects visible light.

Polar Bears have an incredible sense of smell, which is excellent for tracking seals, their favourite food. To catch them, they have exceptional running and swimming skills. Willie loved that their paws were webbed, like a duck, and they used their legs like rudders when swimming up to 10km/h.

Climate change is a big problem for polar bears, as the sea ice melts earlier in the season, reducing their hunting time.

Young polar bear cubs are born in snow dens in November and December. At birth, they are the size of a guinea pig. The mother and her cubs emerge from the den 4-5 months after birth when they are the size of a dog. The cubs then stay with their Mum for two years to learn all the skills they need to survive.

Q q

Queztal

Pharomachnis auriceps

Willie thought the Quetzal was the most beautiful bird he had ever seen. It is bright blue, red, white, and green, and males have long tail feathers (up to a metre long).

The couple in the park had come directly from the mountain forests of Central America, and they would spend much of their time flying around the trees in their enclosure looking for fruits and insects to eat, or they would use their powerful beaks to make holes in the tree trunks. Once they had carved out a hole, they would use it as a nest for one or two eggs, which they would both care for.

In addition to fruits, berries and insects, they also eat small lizards and frogs when given them as a treat by the park rangers. Willie learned from the signs on their enclosure that they had two toes facing forward and two facing backwards so they could hold tight to branches whilst eating.

R r Rhinoceros

Diceros bicornics

Willie spent lots of time with Rinnie, Ronnie and Rannie. They were a similar size to Willie and could run just as fast as he could. Ronnie told him that rhinoceros means 'nose horn', which seemed very appropriate.

Whilst most adult rhinos live apart, the three young brothers were always together, causing mischief – like when they broke open the freezer with their horns to eat all the ice cream in the park cafe. They were herbivores and mostly ate grass and other plants. Their favourite time was dusk and dawn, when they would play with Willie with no visitors or park rangers around.

They had a fantastic sense of smell but couldn't see very far. This meant Willie could surprise them by walking towards them when the wind blew from them to him (often called 'downwind'). He could make them jump as long as they didn't turn around. But if he got it wrong, they would charge at him— it was their defensive super mode.

Every rhino has its unique poo smell and leaves little piles of poo to mark its territory. Quite different to Willie, who liked to spray his poo around all over the place.

The rhinos liked muddy ponds almost as much as Willie and used the mud like sun cream and insect repellent on sunny days.

The older rhinos have horns, and Willie was sad to hear that many rhinos were killed in Africa by poachers who wanted to sell the horns for profit.

S s Sloth

Bradypus

Willie wanted to be a sloth. He loved the idea that you could sleep for 20 hours a day hanging from a tree branch and occasionally move for a meal of leaves. And whilst Willie had a poo several times a day, and more if he was trying to scare off the monkeys, the sloth only had a poo once a week.

This was because sloths live high up in the rainforest trees in South and Central America, moving very slowly. Their top speed is 0.27 km/h when threatened, which is just 4.5m in a minute: how far can you run in one minute? For them, going for a poo was dangerous and meant that they had to move to the bottom of the tree, where there were dangerous predators who might attack them.

Willie asked the sloth in the park why she was a green colour. She explained that it was an algae that grew over her brown hair and provided camouflage so the predators couldn't see her so easily. She also told Willie that her digestive system would take about a week to process the leaves she ate, much longer than hippos and humans.

Willie learned that most sloths live to be about 20 years old in the forests, but in a safari park, they can live almost twice as long without danger from predators.

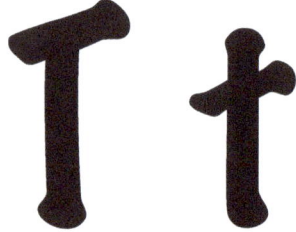

Tortoise

Chelandis nigra

Willie was great friends with Ron, the tortoise. He was impressed that tortoises had lived on Earth when the dinosaurs were alive and that some lived to several hundred years old. Ron was about the size of a small football, but Willie had also seen a giant tortoise the size of a Little Tykes car.

When Ron was scared, for example, when a shadow passed over him, he would withdraw his head, legs, and tail into his firm, rigid shell. The rest of the time, he would wander around, eating grass, weeds, and fruit. His walking speed is about 0.2km/h, but he can 'run' at 0.5km/h when needed, such as when smelling a potential mate in the air.

Being a cold-blooded reptile (unlike warm mammals like Willie and the zookeepers), Ron would sit in the light as soon as the sun rose each day to warm up before walking and eating. On very hot days, his body would overheat, so he needed shade from the trees (or Willie) to cool down.

Ron told Willie that he originally came from an egg buried in the ground and that he needed to hibernate during the winter months, which meant expelling all the processed poo from his body before sleeping. Ron knew many things, and Willie often joked that he 'taught us' many things, which is how he got his name, according to the famous writer Lewis Carroll.

U u Umbrella Bird

Cephalopterus ornatus

The umbrella birds at the safari park were about the same size and colour as crows. They hunted insects and spiders. The park rangers also gave them fruit and berries, which they considered a treat.

Their name was perfect because they had a big tuft of feathers (called a crest) that overhung their eyes, which looked like an umbrella.

They had been brought to the safari park from their home in South America, where humans destroyed many hectares of their rainforest to make way for crops.

Willie used to enjoy watching them in the Spring when the males would make all sorts of noises from their expanding necks (called wattles) and move around trying to attract the smaller female birds. Some of the booming noises sounded just like the noises that Willie could make. Having found a mate, they would build a nest high up in their enclosure and lay just one egg.

Back in their rainforest home, they were hunted by monkeys and snakes, and Willie loved that they would let him know whenever the monkeys escaped from their enclosure by making hippo sounds until Willie answered back.

V v   Vulture

Accipitridae and *Cathartidae*

When Willie was eating cake in the safari park restaurant, he read a leaflet that said there were over twenty types of vultures.

The 'old world' vultures lived in Africa, Asia, and Europe. They ate their food from the dead carcasses of animals they found by flying high above their hunting grounds, looking down with their eyes, and then swooping in as a flock.

And then there were the 'new world' vultures found in North and South America: they found their prey by constantly sniffing the air and then flying towards the smell. They can smell a carcass from two kilometres away with the wind in the right direction. The 'kettle' (the name for a group of vultures in flight) then flies to their target together.

When on the ground, vultures are called a 'committee' and when feeding a 'wake'. Willie liked that hippos were just called a pod; there was no need to remember three names.

Most vultures have a bald head and no feathers on their necks. It is believed that they have evolved this way as they reduce the chance of infection from old meat, blood, and ligaments, which reach into the bones of dead animals. The only trouble is that they can get quite cold when the sun goes down, so they will be seen with their head and neck tucked into their wings. And when too hot, they spread out their wings so that their blood is cooled by any breeze or wind present.

W w

Warthog

Phacochoerus africanus

Warthogs are similar in size and have the same biological family as pigs that humans farm. What distinguishes them is the thick mane on their backs, four large, curled tusks (two up and two down), and 'warts' (protective bumps) on their heads. These warts are most prominent on the males' heads, and they fight each other for the attention of the females when the warmer months start in spring.

When they entered the safari park flower gardens, Willie watched them eat grass, dig out roots of bushes, and even bulbs from the flower beds. They also eat carrion (dead meat), but Willie hadn't witnessed that.

Willie and the warthogs enjoyed the same summer pastime: wallowing in the mud. It kept them cool and helped them avoid the flies.

The warthogs at the safari park had to have a high fence around their enclosure because they could run at over 45km/h and then jump over two metres into the air. Willie could manage about 50cm on a good day. But he was a lot heavier.

Xerus (squirrel)

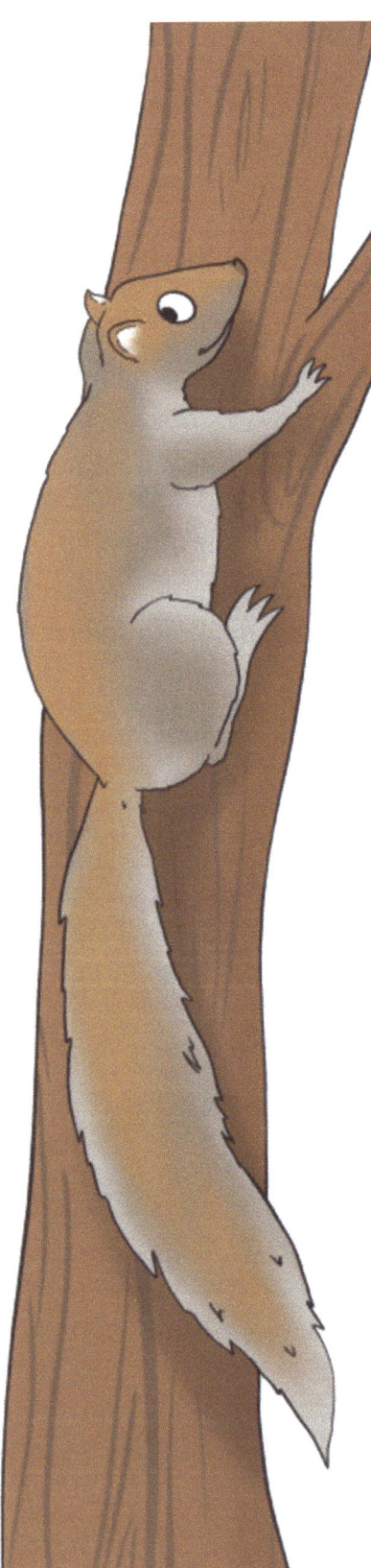

Xerus erythropus

The safari park had an enclosure that housed striped Xerus from Morocco. Willie knew them well because he would often ask Benji, the rabbit, to let them out so they could spy on the monkeys and report on what they were doing. Xerus were small and quickly travelled all over the park, slipping between fences and gates.

Xerus live to be about eleven years old, eating nuts, roots and seeds. Unlike the grey and red squirrels found in Europe, Xerus don't hide or bury their food; they eat it there and then and keep hunting throughout the year. The other difference is that Xerus live in burrows, whereas other squirrels live in drays in trees.

Xerus can run fast when needed, usually when trying to escape from predators such as jackals, snakes and lizards. And if they get overheated in the sun, they use their tails to shade their heads from the sun.

Y y Yak

Bos mutus

Willie was amazed when he first met a Yak and discovered that it could live in temperatures of minus 40 degrees Celsius, having two layers of fur to protect it from the extreme cold. The downside was that it could get very warm in the European summer, and they needed shelter from the sun and a decent breeze, which had to be provided by the safari park rangers using a large fan.

Yaks live in herds of up to a hundred animals and move around eating grass and flowers. They have several stomachs that get all the nutrients from their diet.

When the ground is covered in ice and snow, they use their horns to break through and get at the grass beneath.

They live for about twenty years, mainly in the Himalayas, in the foothills of the world's tallest mountain, Everest. Although some are still wild, many are now domesticated and live with farming families.

The Yak that Willie met was just a bit bigger than him, the size of a large Shire horse like Jack, with shorter legs than a horse. When the yak made noises, they were grunts and squeaks rather than cow mooing sounds that Willie had expected.

Z z

Zebra

Equus quagga

Ziggy the Zebra was great friends with Willie and had such a strong kick that he could score a goal from one end of the football pitch to the other (but always with his back legs, never his weaker front legs).

Zebras live in Africa in groups called Zeal. Each Zeal has a hierarchy led by a male (the Stallion), who leads his Harem (females). Like Willie, they are herbivores and live up to 25 years.

A fantastic thing about the Zebra is that it is one of only a few mammals that can see in colour. This made Willie quite jealous, although he didn't know what colours meant, having not seen them before.

The other fantastic thing is that Zebra sleeps standing up and only goes to sleep if they are close to neighbours, so they can be warned if a predator is nearby.

They pull their ears backwards when angry or stand erect when feeling calm and friendly.

Zebra only have one toe on each foot and can run up to 65 km/h. When being chased by predators, they will run in a zig-zag pattern to try and make it more difficult for the predator to follow them. I wonder if Ziggy uses the zigzag to confuse his opponents, Willie thought.

Each Zebra has a unique pattern of stripes. Like the polar bear, they have black skin with white translucent stripes. The stripes are considered good insect repellents, providing excellent camouflage from lions on the plains of Africa.

A Zebra pregnancy lasts about a year and produces one foal at a time. The mother keeps the foal close to her for the first few days until it becomes used to her unique smell.

www.ingramcontent.com/pod-product-compliance
Lightning Source LLC
Chambersburg PA
CBHW051322110526
44590CB00031B/4443